FACT CAT

STONE AGE TO IRON AGE

Izzi Howell

FACT CAT

Get your paws on this fantastic new mega-series from Wayland!

Join our Fact Cat on a journey of fun learning about every subject under the sun!

Published in paperback in 2016
First published in hardback in 2015
Copyright © Wayland 2015

ISBN: 978 0 7502 9938 1
Dewey Number: 936.1'01-dc23

10 9 8 7 6 5 4 3 2 1

MIX
Paper from responsible sources
FSC
www.fsc.org   FSC® C104740

Wayland is an imprint of Hachette Children's Group
Part of Hodder & Stoughton
Carmelite House
50 Victoria Embankment
London EC4Y 0DZ

An Hachette UK Company
www.hachette.co.uk
www.hachettechildrens.co.uk

A catalogue for this title is available from
the British Library
Printed and bound in China

Produced for Wayland by
White-Thomson Publishing Ltd
www.wtpub.co.uk

Editor: Izzi Howell
Design: Rocket Design (East Anglia) Ltd
Fact Cat illustrations: Shutterstock/Julien Troneur
Other illustrations: Stefan Chabluk
Consultant: Kate Ruttle

Picture and illustration credits:
Corbis: Last Refuge/Robert Harding World Imagery
15, The Print Collector 19; iStock: wittyn11 cover and 11,
fotoVoyager title page and 20; Science Photo Library: Luis
Montanya/Marta Montanya 7 and 8, P.Plailly/E.Daynes 18;
Shutterstock: jps 4l, Jason Benz Bennee 5, Claudio Divizia 9,
Creative Nature Media 10, luri 14t; Thinkstock: Kyslynskyy
6; Wikimedia: Archäologisches Museum Hamburg
(Archaeological Museum Hamburg) 4c, PHGCOM 4r, Portable
Antiquities Scheme 12, Wikimedia 13, Gaius Cornelius 14b,
Dave 16, Sailko 17l, Johnbod 17r, Joseph Martin Kronheim 21.

The author, Izzi Howell, is a writer and editor specialising in children's educational publishing.

The consultant, Kate Ruttle, is a literacy expert and SENCO, and teaches in Suffolk.

FACT CAT FACT

There is a question for you to answer on each spread in this book. You can check your answers on page 24.

CONTENTS

THE STONE, BRONZE AND IRON AGES

The first people arrived in Britain around 750,000 years ago. However, the people living in Britain didn't have a written language until the Romans arrived in 43CE. The time before people in Britain started writing is called British **prehistory**.

Prehistory is divided into three **time periods**. Each period is named after the material that was most commonly used to make tools at that time. Which prehistoric period happened first?

This is a stone axe from the Stone Age – 750,000BCE to 2500BCE.

This is a bronze axe from the Bronze Age – 2500BCE to 800BCE.

This is an iron sword from the Iron Age – 800BCE to around 43CE.

Prehistory lasted for over 750,000 years. Not many prehistoric objects have lasted until modern times, but **archaeologists** are always looking for clues that show us what prehistoric life was like.

Prehistoric objects can teach us about the past. This gold Iron Age bracelet shows us the type of jewellery that rich people wore at that time.

FACT CAT FACT

The people who lived in Britain during the Iron Age are called the Celts. Groups of Celts also lived across Europe. The Celts spoke Celtic languages, similar to modern Welsh or Gaelic.

FOUD AND FARMING

People in Stone Age Britain were hunter-gatherers. They spent their lives moving from place to place, looking for food. They hunted **wild** animals and collected fruit and vegetables.

Wild boar were often hunted by hunter-gatherers. Can you find out if wild boar still live in Britain today?

At the start of the Stone Age, people could hunt woolly rhinos in Britain! Archaeologists have found rhinoceros bones with knife marks, which shows they were hunted and eaten by humans.

Towards the end of the Stone Age, European **settlers** showed people in Britain how to farm. This changed everyday life for people in Britain. They started to live on farms, and had more time for other activities.

On Bronze and Iron Age farms, people planted **crops**, such as wheat and barley. They kept animals for milk and meat.

RULERS AND TRIBES

The **population** of Britain was very small in the Stone Age. People lived in family groups and weren't controlled by a **ruler**.

In Stone Age groups, everyone had a different job. Some people hunted and others prepared food or made tools.

hunting

preparing food

making tools

The population of Britain grew in the Bronze Age. By the Iron Age, small family groups had joined together into **tribes**. Each tribe had its own ruler. Tribes would fight each other for land or **resources**.

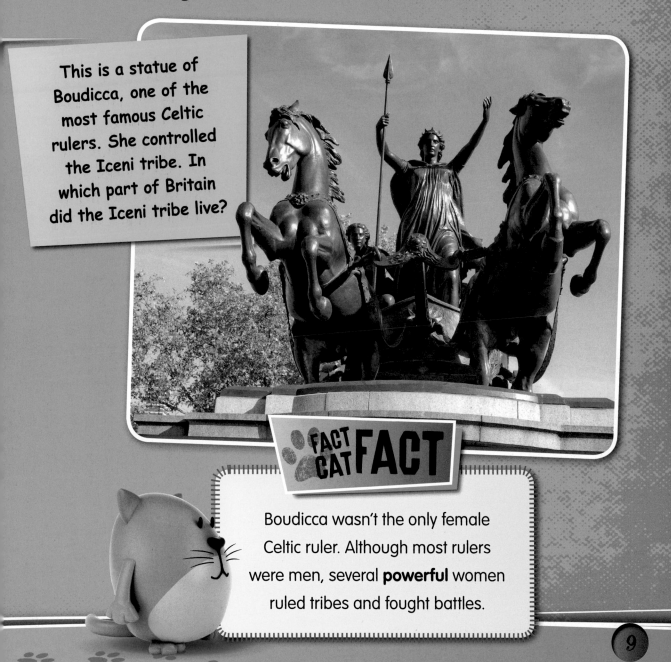

This is a statue of Boudicca, one of the most famous Celtic rulers. She controlled the Iceni tribe. In which part of Britain did the Iceni tribe live?

FACT CAT FACT

Boudicca wasn't the only female Celtic ruler. Although most rulers were men, several **powerful** women ruled tribes and fought battles.

HOUSES

The first Stone Age hunter-gatherers slept in caves as they moved around the country. As people started to stay longer in each place to grow food, they began to build **huts** that would last for several months.

It's likely that Stone Age huts had a wooden **frame**. The frame was covered with animal furs to keep the hut warm.

In the Bronze and Iron Ages, groups of people lived together in small villages. Their houses had walls made from dry mud and sticks and a straw roof. Inside, there was one room where the family slept and cooked.

Most houses in the Bronze and Iron Ages were round, like the houses in this **reconstruction** of an Iron Age village.

FACT CAT FACT

The straw roof of a roundhouse could weigh up to 2 tonnes. That's as much as a hippopotamus! What is another name for a straw roof?

TOOLS

The first tools people made were simple. They were made by hitting stones together until one stone had a sharp edge. It took a long time to cut plants or meat with stone tools.

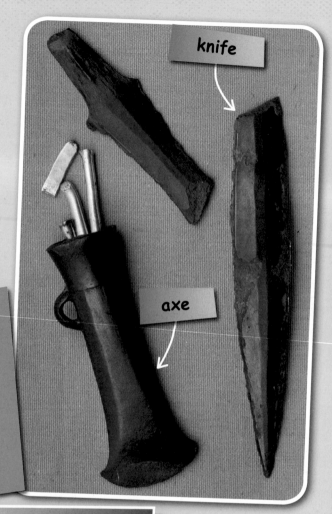

knife

axe

Around 2500BCE, people in Britain learned how to make tools from bronze. Bronze tools, such as this axe and knife, were much stronger and sharper than stone tools.

FACT CAT FACT

A group of people from Europe called the Beakers probably taught people in Britain how to make bronze. How did the Beakers get their name?

Bronze tools made farming much easier. Farmers could grow more food than their villages needed. People started to travel to other parts of Britain to **trade** food and bronze tools.

People learned how to make tools from iron in around 800BCE. These tools were used to harvest crops.

sickle

WEAPONS AND WARS

Stone Age weapons were used mainly for hunting, as fights between people were unusual. As the population of Britain got bigger in the Bronze Age, people started to fight each other more often.

Stone Age weapons, such as arrowheads, were often made out of a stone called flint.

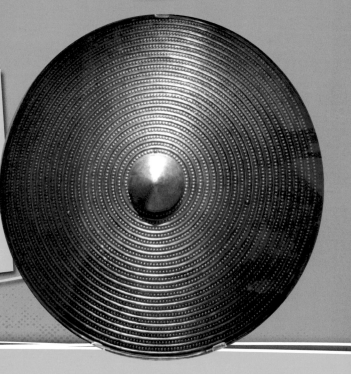

In the Bronze Age, weapons and shields were made from bronze. The decorations on this bronze shield show that it belonged to someone important.

Many Iron Age tribes built high hill forts to **protect** their villages from attacks from other tribes or invaders from different countries. The whole village would live on top of the high ground, and walls would be built around them to keep them safe.

FACT CAT FACT

There are remains of over 3,000 Iron Age hill forts in Britain. Can you find out the names of two of them?

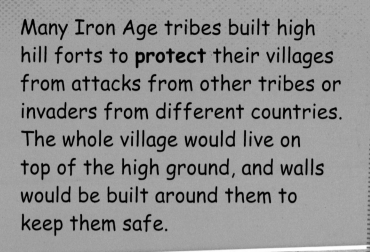

In Iron Age times, there was a hill fort on top of this hill. The edges of the hill have been dug away to make it harder to attack.

ARTS AND CRAFTS

Stone Age people decorated stones and animal bones with pictures. Like artists today, they drew things that they could see around them, such as animals or people.

This picture of a horse's head drawn on a bone is one of the oldest pieces of Stone Age art found in Britain. It's probably about 12,500 years old.

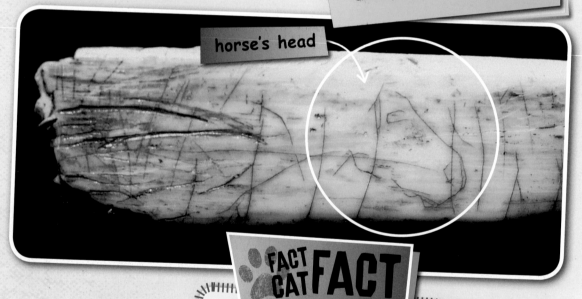

horse's head

FACT CAT FACT

The oldest art found on Earth is a zigzag line carved onto a shell. It is over 400,000 years old!

In the Bronze and Iron Ages, **craftsmen** used metal to make beautiful objects as well as useful tools. Powerful rulers of tribes started carrying expensive decorated jewellery and armour to show how rich they were.

This Bronze Age cape made from gold is known as the Mold Cape. It was probably worn by the ruler of a Bronze Age tribe on special occasions. How did the Mold Cape get its name?

This decorated Iron Age shield is actually made from bronze! The designs on the shield look a bit like birds.

CLOTHES

Stone Age people wore animal skins to keep warm. The skins were sewn together to make clothes using bone needles and thread made from stringy bits of animal meat.

This model shows what Stone Age clothes probably looked like. This man is dressed for hunting, and is carrying a long spear.

By the Bronze Age, people knew how to **weave** wool into cloth. This cloth was made into clothes, such as **tunics** and trousers. Shoes and cloaks were made from **leather**.

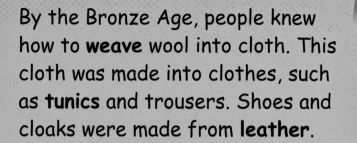

In the Bronze and Iron Ages, most people wore woven tunics, with skirts for women and trousers for men.

tunic

FACT CAT FACT

Some Iron Age warriors wore very few clothes. They used **dye** from a plant to paint their bodies blue. What was the name of this plant?

RELIGION

Large stone circles were built across Britain during the Stone Age. Some of them are still standing today. Most historians think that these circles were used for religious **ceremonies**.

Some stones were brought to Stonehenge from nearly 400km away in west Wales. No one knows how the heavy stones were carried such a long way.

FACT CAT FACT

The largest stones at Stonehenge weigh 50 tonnes. That's as much as the weight of ten adult elephants combined!

In the Iron Age, people thought that gods and goddesses lived in nature. People worshipped and celebrated the different gods and made **sacrifices** to them. Religious men at the time were called druids.

This is a drawing of Iron Age druids. Druids used sickles to gather special plants. Which plant with white berries did druids often pick?

QUIZ Try to answer the questions below. Look back through the book to help you. Check your answers on page 24.

1 Which time period ended around 2500BCE?

a) the Stone Age

b) the Bronze Age

c) the Iron Age

2 People in Stone Age Britain had farms. True or not true?

a) true

b) not true

3 What shape were many houses in the Bronze and Iron Ages?

a) round

b) square

c) rectangular

4 Hill forts were built to protect Iron Age villages. True or not true?

a) true

b) not true

5 Why did Stone Age people wear animal skins?

a) to look good

b) to keep warm

c) to show that they were powerful

6 Druids were religious men. True or not true?

a) true

b) not true

GLOSSARY

archaeologist someone who studies objects left behind by people who lived in the past

BCE (Before the Common Era) before the birth of Christ

CE (Common Era) after the birth of Christ

ceremony a special event

craftsman someone who is skilled at making things by hand

crop a plant that is grown in large numbers/quantities by farmers

dye something which changes the colour of something else

frame the inside structure of an object

hut a small simple building which may not last for a long time

leather animal skins which can be used to make clothes or shoes

population the amount of people living in an area

powerful able to control people and events

prehistory the time before people started writing about history

protect to keep something safe

reconstruction a place that has been built to look the same as it would have done in the past

resource something that people need, such as wood, metal or water

ruler someone who controls a country or an area

sacrifice to kill something to make a god happy in a religious ceremony

settler someone who comes to live in a new country or area

sickle a tool with a curved blade used to cut plants

time period a specific length of time in history

trade to give something to someone, and get something in return

tribe a group of people who live together

tunic a piece of clothing that covers the top part of your body

weave to make cloth by passing threads over and under each other

wild living naturally and not looked after by humans

INDEX

ANSWERS

Pages 4–21

page 4: The Stone Age

page 6: Yes, they do

page 9: East England, close to where Norfolk is today

page 11: A thatched roof

page 12: From their pottery beakers

page 15: Some examples include Danebury and Maiden Castle

page 17: It was found near the town of Mold in Wales

page 19: Woad

page 21: Mistletoe

Quiz answers

1   a) the Stone Age

2   b) not true. They were hunter-gatherers.

3   a) round

4   a) true

5   b) to keep warm

6   a) true